FranklinCovey™

ALSO BY STEPHEN R. COVEY & MANGO MEDIA

The 7 Habits of Highly Effective People - Interactive Edition

The 7 Habits of Highly Effective People - Snapshots Edition

First Things First - Interactive Edition with A. Roger Merrill
and Rebecca R. Merrill

Great Work Great Career - Interactive Edition

ISBN 978-1-63353-270-0

www.franklincovey.com

CONTENTS

INTRODUCTION

Stephen R. Covey was a master teacher.

Millions of people know this. It's not exactly a secret. But what people may not fully understand is that Stephen Covey was a master teacher because he was first a master student. He wasn't born Dr. Stephen R. Covey. As a little kid on the playground, he did not preach the principles of synergy during a particularly intense game of kickball. When he got older, he did not lecture visiting friends about putting first things first as they picked up toys before devouring an afternoon snack. It's an interesting idea. But it did not happen.

He paid attention to the world around him. He asked questions. He sought after new knowledge. And when he found a principle of knowledge that would help him be better, he fully embraced it. You can see this in *The 7 Habits of Highly Effective People*. People asked him all the time: "How? How did you come up with *The 7 Habits*?"

He would simply smile upon hearing the question, take a moment to contemplate it and then answer with impeccable timing: "I didn't." Of course, anyone asking the question was confused by this response. But before a follow-up question could be presented, he delivered the answer.

"I wrote the book," he would answer, "but the principles were known long before me. They are more like natural laws," he would say. "All I did was put them together to synthesize them for people."

Conversations were his classroom. When you met him, he would envelope you in his strong handshake, his inviting presence. Whether you were a family member, a close friend, or an acquaintance—even if you bumped into him casually—you could spend the next few hours engaged in a meaningful conversation about family, friends, and work….life.

The principles he shared were timeless. He spent well over thirty years studying, practicing and refining the principles presented within *The 7 Habits of Highly Effective People*. He was always looking to teach these principles, to make them comprehendible and accomplishable.

Because he understood that never before has the world been so big. Opportunities unlike anything we have seen before await the next generation. But never before has the world been so small. Technology has linked us together in powerful and sometime dangerous ways. The amount of knowledge at our fingertips is incalculable. With this grand amount of information it becomes increasingly difficult to know what's right and what's wrong.

As you interact with the world, what questions do you ask? There are some basic ones that may come to mind such as: "Why is he driving so slowly in the left lane?"

That question seems to be asked a lot, especially in the morning and late afternoon. Naturally, a favorite question of parents tends to be: "What were you thinking?"

Those are not the questions we should dwell on, especially since the answers to those questions are never very good.

- What questions can you ask to keep learning?

- What knowledge can you gain by asking the right questions?

- What changes can you make by embracing the knowledge that you discover?

- What discipline is needed to make those changes a part of your true character?

There is no effectiveness without discipline and there is no discipline without character. And there is no character without first starting and asking questions.

Stephen R. Covey passed away in 2012. But he will never stop teaching. What you'll find on the following pages are a collection of his thoughts on topics that relate to living an effective life.

He wholeheartedly believed that if everyone in the world lived by *The 7 Habits*, that the world would be a better place. Jim Collins said a few years back that "no person lasts forever, but books and ideas can endure."

We hope that as you move forward through these pages, you will discover the message that goes beyond a simple lesson.

We hope that the message he crafted all those years ago continues to resonate with you and your friends and family.

--Stephen Covey's colleagues

THE BEGINNING

Inhale. Exhale. Repeat.

Geoff was going to do this. Really. For a few minutes he was going to unplug. He was going to enjoy this fabulous weather. He was going to sit on this ridiculously uncomfortable bench. He was going to revel in the sounds of his daughter, Molly, playing at the park.

He was not going to check his cellphone. He was not going to keep one ear constantly tuned in for the PING! of his phone announcing a new message. He was not. . .

PING!

Well, just because he heard it, didn't mean that he had to look at it. Or even respond to it. Unless it was his spouse. Unless his spouse needed something. Unless it was urgent. He didn't want to get in trouble for not responding. Perhaps he should just look. . .

Geoff stopped midreach when he heard a little voice whisper behind his shoulder. "Daddy! Daddy!"

Geoff turned around to figure out why Molly was whispering. This was Molly. She thought whispering was yelling slowly and with more spit. Something was definitely up.

"Daddy, look! A ladybug!"

Indeed, crawling around Molly's hands was a little spotted lady-bug, looking for a way out from its temporary concave prison.

"Daddy, count her dots, and we can find out how old she is!"

"By her dots?" Daddy asked. "I don't think that's true."

"Daddy! My teacher said to count the dots. Ladybugs get new dots every year on their birthday!"

Geoff was just about to insist, a little more firmly, that it just wasn't true. But he was spared the fight—where Molly would once again insist her teacher was a genius and her Dad absolutely was not—when the ladybug finally remembered that it had wings and flew away from Molly's little hands.

"I wonder why they do that?" Geoff asked.

"Do what?"

Geoff smiled. "Why do ladybugs take so long to remember they have wings? They get stuck. They can fly away anytime but don't. Probably because people forget sometimes, too."
"Forget what, Daddy?"

"That we have a power within us. Like flying."
Molly giggled. "Daddy, you can't fly."

Geoff sighed. No, he couldn't. But it would be amazing. And it certainly would cut down on his grueling commute time.

"Miss Molly, don't you know Moms and Dads can do amazing things? Maybe we can't fly. We're still really cool. But sometimes we forget."

"Why do you forget?"

"We get a little lost, I guess," Geoff answered. "Remember when the ladybug was wandering all over your hands, back and forth, back and forth? People do that, too. They get a little stuck. And they think that's normal. Because there's another bug doing exactly the same thing. But we don't crawl on little girls' hands. We call it work and meetings and conference calls and even kids soccer games."

"You get stuck at my soccer games?" Molly asked.

"No, at soccer games I remember my wings. I watch you play and excel, and I remember. I remember I can fly. Because I had you. And you're amazing."

"Daddy," Molly whispered. Loudly and with a great quantity of spit. "Daddy, do you think I have wings, too?"

Seeing is the challenge.
The lessons are all around us.

- STEPHEN R. COVEY

Stephen R. Covey believed the greatest lessons could be learned by simply looking to nature. In fact, he used to offer leadership seminars in natural settings, and he promised the people who attended:

If you will open yourself to the natural environment, the people around you, and timeless principles, you will find personal and specific answers to the leadership challenges and opportunities you face.

He called this the Sundance Promise, named after Robert Redford's resort Sundance, Utah, and the location of many leadership retreats.

Just like Geoff taught Molly a quick lesson based on the peculiarities of a ladybug, Dr. Covey believed that nature is always teaching great truths, if we are willing to be open to learn.

The following pages contain timeless principles of truth from Dr. Covey, especially relating to the life-truths everyone can learn from nature. Each message is a direct quote from him and will teach a fundamental lesson on how to embrace a more effective life.

But no matter the strength and beauty of the message, it will be useless unless it is put into action. It will be useless unless it is embraced. As Dr. Covey was fond of saying: "To know and not to do is not to know."

A more effective life is *not* a more efficient life. This book does not share how to live a better life with the least amount of personal effort. This book shares how to live a more effective life by choosing to:

> **• Let Nature Teach You About Natural Laws:** Recognize and model principles found in the laws of nature;

- **Let Nature Increase Your Self-Awareness:** Examine personal paradigms to be more aware of personal paradigms and take personal responsibility actions;

- **Let Nature Teach You How To Nurture Relationships:** Seek opportunities to be leaders in your personal life and in relationships by putting a daily focus on people, not things;

- **Let Nature Guide Your Choices:** Find power by making correct choices;

- **Let Nature Show You How To Celebrate Diversity:** Celebrate the differences around you.

This book is not designed to be simply read; it's designed to be experienced. The message is powerful, practical, and immediately applicable and communicated through quotes, experiences and infographics.

At the end of this book, you will find the Personal Journal: Experiencing a More Effective Life. If you wish to incorporate what you read, the personal journal can help. By asking introspective questions, we hope to provide you with a tool to sculpt out the steps to reach that desired change. Please take advantage of every single page.

This entire book is designed to help readers on the path to a more effective life. Walk with us.

CHAPTER I

Let Nature Teach You
About Natural Laws

SUCCESS

I don't care how successful or wealthy you become or how many accomplishments you achieve, the greatest feeling you can get is to be able to go back to the purest form of nature, to walk on the grass, to be around the trees.

Nature gets you away from the stress, from all the busy-ness you create in your life when you go everywhere to go nowhere.

You're able to think and be more introspective.

You get to look within yourself and create a peaceful environment.

And without that quality time, you don't think deeply.

You don't get a chance to really plan.

You just react, and then you're in crisis management all the time and you make mistakes.

You make quick decisions without planning or preparation.

You don't really think about the vision you want and how it's going to play out.

The reality is that nature is where we're most at home.

That's where life's most basic realities are clear.

It's only when we try to feel at home in an artificial world, thinking we're in control, looking at life through a mechanical paradigm, trying to "fix" other people and find fulfillment in checking off "to do's" that we end up cynical and embittered, running faster and faster—like a rat on a wheel.

As the saying goes, "fish discover water last."

SEEKING CONTEXT

I've learned to time things so that I am driving with a beautiful sunset off to the west as I drive home.

It calms me.

It gives me a perspective.

I think, "There is a hideous traffic jam in front of me. There are trucks on either side of me. This is a mess and I can't believe any good will ever come of it.

But look at that phenomenal sunset! Look at those clouds.

Look at the reflection on the mountains.

Look at how it makes the snow sparkle on the mountains."

It puts things in context.

CHANGE IS A VITAL PART OF LIFE

Nature teaches that change is a vital part of life.

Seeds change. Seasons change. Weather changes.
People change.

We are part of a dynamic, growing,
ever-changing environment.

Through change, we create better organizations, more
productive teams, more harmonious families, better selves.

The problem comes when we try to create change as
though we live in a static environment. We try to fix people,
install programs, or repair relationships, as though they
were isolated broken parts in some mechanical whole.

THE SUNDANCE PROMISE

If you will open yourself to the natural environment, the people around you, and timeless principles, you will find personal and specific answers to the leadership challenges and opportunities you face.

THE ANECDOTE OF THE BOY SCOUT

The story goes as follows : "In the distant days when I was a boy scout, I had a troop leader who was an ardent woodsman and naturalist. He would take us on hikes not saying a word, and then challenge us to describe what we had observed: trees, plants, birds, wildlife, everything. Invariably we hadn't seen a quarter as much as he had, nor half enough to satisfy him."

"Creation is all around you," he would cry, waving his arms in vast inclusive circles. "But you're keeping it out. Don't be a buttoned-up person! Stop wearing your raincoat in the shower!"

LEARNING FROM TODAY

A friend once told me that he believes that every living thing, whether it's a plant, an animal, or an insect, has its own natural habitat. And if it wants to be healthy and normal, it has to live within that environment.

As he put it, "a human being's natural habitat is a garden." It is in the garden that we are biologically realistic.

When the eye sees the branches of a tree move slightly in the wind or the clouds move silently through the sea of space, or when the ear hears the sounds of rushing water or birds singing, it helps to tranquilize the soul.

Tranquility leads to dynamic creative thinking and creative communication.

"But human beings now are made to live with the sounds of telephones, engines, sirens, and whistles. Their eyes are forced to look upon a concrete world, car exhaust, power poles, telephone lines, clutter, and junk—all of which produce tension instead of tranquility."

The key is to learn from nature and the world around you. To learn from today.

IN NATURE, THERE ARE SEASONS.

There are times of preparing and planting, times of watering and nurturing, times—often very intense times—of harvest.

Although some are seasons of imbalance, each season contributes to the balance of the whole.

Our lives and our organizations also have seasons.

A new baby, a new business, a new challenge may create seasons of imbalance.

But effectively handled, even these seasons of imbalance help to create the balance of the whole.

Throughout your pursuit of an effective life there will be opposition.

Nature teaches the value of opposition and challenge. The turbulent stream purifies the water.

By pushing against its cocoon, the butterfly gains sufficient strength to fly. In our own lives and organizations, exercising our muscles—physical, mental, or moral—gives us strength and prevents atrophy.

The leader learns to learn from the challenges, failures, and problems of life to improve life.

THE LAW OF THE FARM

Consider the Law of the Farm. The same law that tells you it's ludicrous to think you can goof off all spring, play all summer, throw a bunch of seeds in the ground at the beginning of fall, and reap a bountiful harvest two weeks later also tells you there's no way you're going to neglect planning and preparation, avoid building relationships, and side-step problems, and end up with a strong, effective family or organization.

It also tells you that whatever you sow, you're going to reap. If, as a leader, you sow seeds of mistrust through dishonesty, backbiting, using people, or playing political games, you're never going to reap the benefits of a high trust culture in the long run. You may experience some apparent short-term results, but they will never endure.

In the long term, The Law of the Farm will govern. You simply cannot violate with impunity the laws that govern growth. In other words, if you plant weeds, you're never going to harvest peas.

Now, there will still be unknowns. Like the farmer, you can't predict exactly what will happen to your crop every year. Sometimes the unpredictability of weather and other conditions will change the time of harvest. Something in the environment may even destroy the crop. But still you learn that if you keep preparing the soil, planting, nurturing, and doing all you can to be a wise steward, over time you will reap what you sow.

Though the individual events can't always be predicted, the pattern can be predicted. If you think in terms of principles, are true to principles, and exercise faith in the results, they will eventually come to pass.

LESSONS FROM THE GARDEN

My garden taught me about being a good friend and a good relative. It taught me how you have to nurture relationships. It also taught me that in order to enjoy the fruits in life, you must work.

The work is hard. Sometimes it is difficult to see progress. But seeds do grow and bear fruit. I think that working in the garden, and associating that experience so closely with my education and philosophy, has helped me to understand and appreciate everything I encounter in life.

CHAPTER 2

Let Nature Increase Your Self-Awareness

ULTIMATE FREEDOM

Our ultimate freedom is the right and power to decide
how anybody or anything outside ourselves will affect us.

OBJECTIVE INTROSPECTION

Until we see ourselves from the outside objectively, we will automatically project our motives onto other people.

THE HAVE'S AND THE BE'S

One way to determine which circle our concern is in is to distinguish between the have's and the be's.

THE CIRCLE OF CONCERN IS FILLED WITH THE HAVE'S:

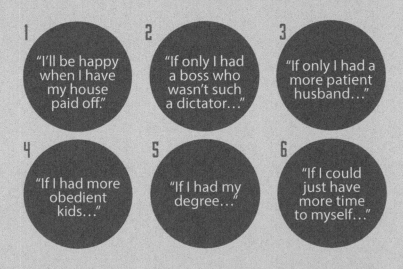

1 "I'll be happy when I have my house paid off."

2 "If only I had a boss who wasn't such a dictator..."

3 "If only I had a more patient husband..."

4 "If I had more obedient kids..."

5 "If I had my degree..."

6 "If I could just have more time to myself..."

THE CIRCLE OF INFLUENCE IS FILLED WITH THE BE'S

1 I can be more patient

2 I can be wise

3 I can be loving

IT'S THE CHARACTER FOCUS

Anytime we think the problem is "out there," that thought is the problem. We empower what's out there to control us. The change paradigm is "outside-in"—what's out there has to change before we can change.

AN EFFECTIVE LIFE

I've spent my entire life studying what it takes to be effective. Personal and interpersonal effectiveness are vital. But they are just the price of entry in today's environment. The call today is for leadership greatness. Becoming a great leader is a journey and like all worthwhile journeys, it will be filled with significant challenges as well as exhilarating triumphs. Welcome to the journey.

LEADER — OR VICTIM

That's essentially the choice we all face today. And more
than ever before, there's not much middle ground. Either we
lead effectively—in our businesses, our families, our communities, even our personal lives—or we're tossed about by
the circumstances that surround us.

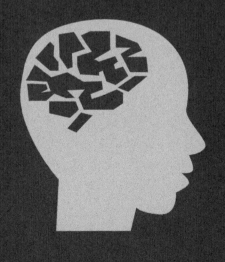

Each habit depends on the development of your proactive muscles. Each puts the responsibility on you to act. If you wait to be acted upon, you will be acted upon. And growth and opportunity consequences attend either road.

UNDER ATTACK

You might be asking , "How can I choose positive synergy when others are attacking me?"

Although you can't control the paradigms of others, you can be synergistic within yourself even in the midst of a very adversarial environment.

You can choose not to be offended, you can seek out your adversary and listen with empathy.

You will enlarge your own perspective and you might find that empathy alone can diffuse the conflict.

DISCIPLINE COMES FROM WITHIN

If you are an effective manager of yourself, your discipline comes from within; it is a function of your independent will.

You are a disciple, a follower, of your own deep values and their source. And you have the will, the integrity, to subordinate your feelings, your impulses, your moods to those values.

INTRODUCING THE
LEADER IN EVERYONE

I do not define a leader as one of the few who end up in big leadership roles and positions. We are used to thinking of leaders as people with titles, like CEO or president.

This view of leadership is an artifact of the Industrial Age and we are long past that hierarchal line of thinking. I am talking about the ability to lead your own life, to lead among your friends, to be a leader in your own family; to be the active and creative force of your own life.

True leaders define success on their own terms. They don't wait for others to define it for them because they see themselves as powerful and gifted.

They compete against no one but themselves. In economic terms, they are the only providers of what they can provide so they can auction their talents to the highest bidder.

These leaders create their own future and they have respect for self and for others.

THE TWO ADDITIONAL UNIQUE **HUMAN ENDOWMENTS THAT ENABLE US TO** EXPAND OUR PROACTIVITY **& TO EXERCISE** PERSONAL LEADERSHIP **IN OUR LIVES ARE:**

1. *imagination*

THROUGH IMAGINATION

- WE CAN VISUALIZE THE UNCREATED WORLDS OF POTENTIAL THAT LIE WITHIN US AND

2. *conscience*

THROUGH CONSCIENCE
- WE CAN COME IN CONTACT WITH UNIVERSAL LAWS OR PRINCIPLES WITH OUR OWN SINGULAR TALENTS AND AVENUES OF CONTRIBUTION.

COMBINED WITH SELF-AWARENESS, THESE TWO ENDOWMENTS EMPOWER US TO WRITE OUR OWN SCRIPT.

Because we already live with many scripts that have been handed to us, the process of writing our own script is actually more a process of "rescripting," or paradigm shifting—of changing some of the basic paradigms that we already have. As we recognize the ineffective scripts, the incorrect or incomplete paradigms within us, we can proactively begin to rescript ourselves.

CHAPTER 3

Let Nature Teach You How
To Nurture Relationships

THE ONE

Caring about the one works because it's a paradigm focused on people, not things; it's focused on relationships, not schedules; it's focused on effectiveness, not efficiency; it's focused on personal leadership, not resource management.

SACRIFICE

To be effective we need to sacrifice our pride and seek humility. That's the nature of the sacrifice required today—the sacrifice of ego. We need to enter into our relationships with each other with a spirit of mutual respect.

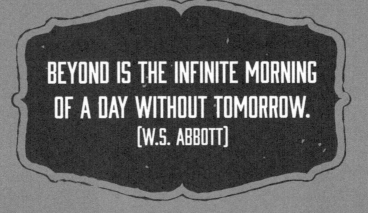

BEYOND IS THE INFINITE MORNING
OF A DAY WITHOUT TOMORROW.
(W.S. ABBOTT)

When I look upon the tombs of the great, every emotion of envy dies in me; when I read the epitaphs of the beautiful, every inordinate desire goes out; when I meet with the grief of parents upon a tombstone, my heart melts with compassion;

when I see the tomb of the parents themselves,
I consider the vanity of grieving for those whom
we must quickly follow;

when I see kings lying by those who deposed
them, when I consider rival wits placed side by
side, or the holy men that divided the world with
their contests and disputes, I reflect with sorrow
and astonishment on the little competitions,
factions, and debates of mankind.

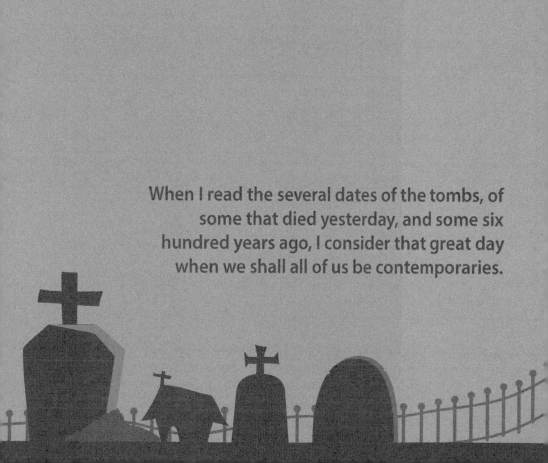

When I read the several dates of the tombs, of some that died yesterday, and some six hundred years ago, I consider that great day when we shall all of us be contemporaries.

LOOK FIRST TO YOURSELF

To improve your relationships, don't look to others to change and don't look to easy shortcuts.

Look to yourself. Be honest with yourself first—the roots of your problems are spiritual, and so are the root solutions.

Build your character and your relationships on the bedrock of principles.

TRUST

Trust is the glue of life. It's the most essential ingredient in effective communication. It's the foundational principle that holds all relationships.

TEMPERED JUDGMENT

We judge ourselves by our intentions and others by their actions.

You might be able to buy someone's hand or back, but you can never buy someone's heart, mind, and spirit. These are volunteered only.

WALLS & RELATIONSHIPS

In this world, the most challenging walls are not between countries but between people. These walls are mostly invisible but they form barriers to trust, communication, and creativity. In today's environment, we simply can't afford these walls.

Imagine the incalculable costs to people and organizations when sales and marketing don't get along, when there is mistrust between labor and management, or when people feel they can't be open and honest resulting in office politics, back biting, or micromanagement.

The key in tearing down these walls is found in practicing Habit 4, Think Win-Win; Habit 5, Seek First to Understand, Then to be Understood; and Habit 6, Synergize.

People need the internal strength to think "we" not "me." They need to understand, not to reply. And when they deeply believe in 3rd Alternatives, that there is truly something better out there just waiting to be created; marvelous things

can happen. This could happen in your organization or in your life. It can happen in any relationship and, you know, all it takes is one person.

Which walls need to be torn down in your relationships?

FAMILY

LIKE YOUR FAMILY, YOUR PATH WILL
BE PERSONAL *AND* UNIQUE.

EVERYONE'S IS.

That's what creates synergy and joy in relationships and sharing.

We all travel from different paths.

POSITIVE CHANGE

The business, the community, the family, or even the individual—is a complex, highly interrelated ecological system.

Each part has a living attachment to every other part. Change in any part affects all parts. When we learn to see leadership problems in terms of living systems, it dramatically changes the way we deal with them. For the effective leader, change is a friend, a companion, a powerful tool, the basis of growth.

Creating positive change is what leadership is all about.

EMPATHIC LISTENING AND CORRECTING MISUNDERSTANDINGS

I remember writing one time in a room on the north shore of Oahu, Hawaii. There was a soft breeze blowing, and so I had opened two windows—one at the front and one at the side—to keep the room cool. I had a number of papers laid out, chapter by chapter, on a large table.

Suddenly, the breeze started picking up and blowing my papers about. I remember the frantic sense of loss I felt because things were no longer in order, including unnumbered pages, and I began rushing around the room trying desperately to put them back.

Finally, I realized it would be better to take ten seconds and close one of the windows.

Empathic listening takes time, but it doesn't take anywhere near as much time as it takes to back up and correct misunderstandings when you're already miles down the road, to redo, to live with unexpressed and unsolved problems, to deal with the results of not giving people psychological air.

A discerning empathic listener can quickly read what's happening down deep, and can show such acceptance, such understanding, that other people feel safe to open up layer after layer until they get to that soft inner core where the problem really lies.

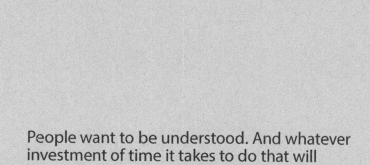

People want to be understood. And whatever investment of time it takes to do that will bring much greater returns of time.

CHAPTER 4

Let Nature Guide Your Choices

COURAGE AND INTEGRITY

We need great courage to lead our lives by correct principles
and to have integrity in the moment of choice.

CHOOSE TO MOVE FORWARD

We live too much out of our memories, too little out of our imaginations—too much on what is or has been, not enough on what can be. That's like trying to drive forward by looking in the rearview mirror.

CARRY YOUR OWN WEATHER

What does it mean to see and listen to nature? And what does it mean to carry your own weather?

PICTURE THIS.
IT'S MONDAY MORNING
AND IT'S RAINING.

A grey melancholy day. On a day like this maybe we can be excused for **feeling grey** and **melancholy ourselves.**

We get into a mood and **the whole day seems to go badly.**

DON'T YOU FEEL BETTER WHEN THE WEATHER OUTSIDE IS GREAT?

But what if you could carry your own weather within you.

When you carry your weather within you, you can **choose** to be consistent regardless of how people treat you. That's what it means to carry your own weather, to be **proactive.**

Being **reactive** is the opposite of being proactive. Being reactive is not taking responsibility for your own life. You always see yourself as a victim of the weather, of your moods, of someone who has it in for you.

We have the power and the freedom to choose. We have the power to create our own weather each day.

What will you choose?

WHO AM I?

I am not a product of my circumstances.
I am a product of my decisions.

CHANGE IS CONSTANT, COMPLEX, AND OFTEN RAPID.

WE CAN'T CONTROL IT.

When we try, it becomes frightening, threatening.

BUT WE CAN LEARN TO UNDERSTAND IT, TO WORK IN HARMONY WITH IT, TO INFLUENCE IT, EVEN TO CULTIVATE IT.

CHOICE

Choice is the summum bonum of human capacity. It empowers us to deal effectively with change and change-lessness. Though human beings are not the only entities in nature that have a choice, it's clear that at least two things about human choice are unique.

The first is that humans have the widest scope of choice. At the same time, they are capable of the most degrading and the most beautiful and uplifting acts in all of nature.

The second is that humans have moral choice. It is the scope and nature of human choice that give us the responsibility of respectful stewardship with regard to the rest of creation.

Our ability to choose affirms that each of us is a leader.

REACTIVE

IN THE GREAT LITERATURE OF ALL PROGRESSIVE SOCIETIES,

LOVE = VERB.

REACTIVE PEOPLE MAKE LOVE A *feeling.*

REACTIVE PEOPLE ARE DRIVEN BY = FEELINGS

HOLLYWOOD SCRIPTED US
TO BELIEVE THAT WE ARE

1. NOT RESPONSIBLE,
2. WE ARE A PRODUCT OUR FEELINGS.

BUT THE HOLLYWOOD SCRIPT ≠ REALITY.

IF OUR FEELINGS CONTROL OUR ACTIONS, IT IS BECAUSE WE HAVE

1. ABDICATED OUR RESPONSIBILITY &
2. EMPOWERED THEM TO DO SO.

PROACTIVE PEOPLE MAKE LOVE A VERB.

LOVE IS SOMETHING YOU DO.

CHOICE & TIMELESS PRINCIPLES

Our ability to choose affirms that each of us is a leader. Every day we make choices that affect the direction of our lives, our families, our organizations, our communities. When choices are made with little or no understanding of natural law, they tend to be simplistic, reactionary, myopic, or egotistical. The cost is extreme.

At the core, almost every personal or organizational failure can be traced to poor decision-making. But when we learn to make choices based on timeless principles—to handle change and create change based on changeless natural laws—we create positive results. Our choices reflect wisdom and lead to contribution. We recognize that others, too, have choice. We tend to lead in ways that respect that choice— ways that release human potential rather than trying to control behavior.

For leaders, choice is where the rubber meets the road.

UNDERSTANDING TRANSFORMATIONS AND CHANGES

To effectively work with change, we need to understand it, to respect it.

A farmer may not understand every biochemical reaction that causes something to grow, but the more he understands the natural processes of planting, nurturing, and growth, the more productive he becomes.

THE CONSCIOUS CHOICE

So how can we learn to make better choices?

We can choose to value principles.

We can choose to look beneath the thin veneer of social conditioning and deep into the true nature of life and leadership.

We can look for principles, seek to really understand and apply them, and live in harmony with them.

Principles control consequences; values control behavior.

The more our values are in harmony with principles, the better decisions we will make… and the more inner peace we will have.

VISUALIZATION AND AFFIRMATION

I can use my **right brain power** of **visualization** to write an "**affirmation**" that will help me become more congruent with my **deeper values** in my daily life.

A GOOD *AFFIRMATION* HAS 5 BASIC INGREDIENTS:

it is:

PERSONAL

POSITIVE

VISUAL

PRESENT TENSE

EMOTIONAL

So I might write
something like this:

"IT IS DEEPLY SATISFYING (EMOTIONAL) THAT I (PERSONAL) RESPOND (PRESENT TENSE) WITH WISDOM, LOVE, FIRMNESS, AND SELF-CONTROL (POSITIVE) WHEN MY CHILDREN MISBEHAVE."

CHAPTER 5

Let Nature Show You How To
Celebrate Diversity

WHERE DO WE GET OUR STRENGTH?

Strength lies in differences, not in similarities.

THE FAMILY IS THE ULTIMATE EXPRESSION OF SYNERGY.

There is a miracle in the transformational, intimate connection that can happen in marriage.

The newborn is the greatest synergistic marvel. A baby is by nature a unique blend of both parents.

Family conflicts are the most heart-breaking of all of life's toughest problems.

This is a great irony.

At home we can experience the most sublime synergies and joys or the deepest distress. I believe that no other success in life can compensate for failure at home. Sometimes marriages end for good reasons, but far more often they end because husbands and wives get discouraged because of their differences. Incompatibility is cited most often as the reason for divorce. The word 'incompatibility' can cover a range of problems: financial, emotional, social, sexual, and more. But usually incompatibility comes down to resentment of differences rather than valuing differences.

SYNERGY IS NOT JUST RESOLVING THE CONFLICT OR COMING TO COMPROMISE.

When we get to synergy, we transcend the conflict.

We go beyond to something new, something that excites everyone with fresh promise and transforms the future.

Synergy is better than my way or your way.
Synergy is a miracle.

It is all around us. It is a fundamental at work throughout the natural world. Redwood trees mingle their roots to stand strong against the wind, and grow to incredible heights. Birds in the V formation can fly nearly twice as far as a lone bird can because of the updraft created by the flapping of their wings. The whole is greater and better than the sum of the parts.

EXPERIENCING REAL SYNERGY

Once people have experienced real synergy they are never quite the same again. They know the possibility of having other such mind-expanding adventures in the future.

Often attempts are made to recreate a particular synergistic experience, but this seldom can be done.

However, the essential purpose behind creative work can be recaptured. Like the Far Eastern philosophy, "We seek not to imitate the masters, rather we seek what they sought." We seek not to imitate past creative synergistic experiences, rather we seek new ones around new and different and sometimes higher purposes.

SYNERGY AND COMMUNICATION

Synergy is exciting. Creativity is
exciting. It's phenomenal what
openness and communication can
produce. The possibilities of truly
significant gain, of significant
improvement, are so real that it's
worth the risk some openness entails.

ANOTHER PERSON'S HEART

I belong to an international forum devoted to building a better relationship between the West and the world's Islamic community. This forum includes some of the world's leading diplomats.

Not too long ago, they invited me to one of their forum meetings to teach them about the mindset and practices of Synergy and thinking 3rd Alternatives. We spent a few days together, learning and practicing principles of impactful listening and skills for truly understanding each person. Each person was challenged to really listen deeply, to open themselves to contrary views, and to feel another person's heart.

This was one of the most profound experiences of my life. As we went through this process, I could see that this distinguished group was totally transformed. People who are on different sides on almost every issue: cultural, social, religious, and more, came to understand each other, respect each other and even love each other. One of the diplomats

told me she had never seen anything so powerful and rev-
olutionary in her life, and that this philosophy could totally
revolutionize international diplomacy.

TREASURE DIFFERENCES

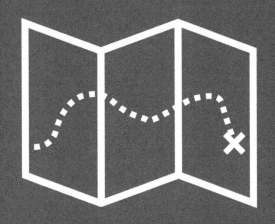

Great marriages arise only when the partners treasure their differences.

For them, the cultures, quirks, talents, strengths, reflexes, and instincts each partner brings into the marriage becomes sources of appreciation, delight, and creativity.

For example, a husband's impatience might make him terrible at tracking the finances, but his spontaneity makes him fun. The wife's reserve frustrates her husband from time to time, but her aristocratic manner charms him and fills him with awe.

And because they cherish each other so much, they are together a unique blend of joy and dignity. Because of their ability to celebrate differences, they create their own unique and precious family culture.

WHEN PEOPLE ARRIVE AT SYNERGY THEIR HEARTS ARE UNDERSTOOD.

At that point their minds become open, creative, and courageous. Defensiveness is removed, fear dissipates, and creativity emerges.

You reach a tipping point where people will no longer accept the unacceptable and move forward to an abundant future together.

We have to stop our ways and stop the destruction. The sheer loss of lives and the devastation inflicted on so many can be stopped. This begins with each of us in our own circles of influence, whether that is in our home, our work, or in our community. We can be examples and create peace in the world. And we grow our influence to help others discover peace.

INTERRELATIONSHIPS

In nature, everything is related to everything else. Consider the complex interrelationship of the food chain, the microorganisms in the soil that allow plants to live, the effect of photosynthesis— of light transforming plant chlorophyll into sugar, creating food for other living things. Anything beyond a casual glance at nature begins to reveal complex levels of interrelationship.

The problem for us as leaders comes when we look at our organization in terms of mechanical, isolated parts instead of as an organic, highly interrelated whole.

Nature teaches us that businesses, families, and communities are also complex ecosystems, and that what happens in one part affects all parts. It also helps us to realize that every individual is important, and that each contributes to the welfare of all.

STEPHEN R. COVEY was an internationally respected leadership authority, family expert, teacher, organizational consultant, and author who dedicated his life to teaching principle-centered living and leadership to build both families and organizations. He earned an M.B.A. from Harvard University and a doctorate from Brigham Young University, where he was a professor of organizational behavior and business management and also served as director of university relations and assistant to the president.

Dr. Covey was the author of several acclaimed books, including the international bestseller, *The 7 Habits of Highly Effective People*, which was named the #1 Most Influential Business Book of the Twentieth Century and one of the top-ten most influential management books ever. It has sold more than 25 million copies in more than 40 languages throughout the world. Other bestsellers include *First Things First, Principle-Centered Leadership, The 7 Habits of Highly Effective Families, The 8th Habit,* and *The 3rd Alternative* bringing the combined total to more than 30 million books sold.

As a father of nine and grandfather of forty-three, he received the 2003 Fatherhood Award from the National Fatherhood Initiative, which he said was the most meaningful award he ever received.

Other awards given to Dr. Covey include the Thomas More College Medallion for continuing service to humanity, Speaker of the Year in 1999, the Sikh's 1998 International Man of Peace Award, the 1994 International Entrepreneur of the Year Award, and the National Entrepreneur of the Year Lifetime Achievement Award for Entrepreneurial Leadership. Dr. Covey was recognized as one of Time magazine's 25 Most Influential Americans and received seven honorary doctorate degrees.

Dr. Covey was the cofounder and vice chairman of Franklin-Covey Co., the leading global professional services firm, with offices in 123 countries. FranklinCovey shares Dr. Covey's vision, discipline, and passion to inspire, lift, and provide tools for change and growth.

PERSONAL JOURNAL

Experiencing An Effective Life

At the beginning of this book the challenge was presented to move beyond simply reading this book. The challenge was to experience it, to embrace it, to begin walking the path to embracing a more effective life.

This is exactly where you can begin to embrace the thoughts presented by Dr. Covey.

As you've read the messages, some ideas may have been sparked. The purpose of this personal journal is to not lose those ideas—to not lose those sparks—but to turn them into a roaring fire.

There is work involved in this personal journal.

Did we lose you?

It's not mind numbing work. It's not stressful work. It's not even tedious work.

But as you move through this personal journal, it could spark a change. In fact, it could change everything.

So let's get started by examining the five themes in developing an effective life.

Let Nature Teach You About Natural Laws:
Recognize and model principles found in the laws of nature.

Let Nature Increase Your Self-Awareness:
Examine personal paradigms to be more aware of personal paradigms and take personal responsibility for actions.

Let Nature Teach You How To Nurture Relationships:
Seek opportunities to be leaders in your personal life and relationships by putting a daily focus on people, not things.

Let Nature Guide Your Choices:
Find power by making correct choices.

Let Nature Show You How to Celebrate Diversity:
Celebrate the differences around you.

LET NATURE TEACH YOU ABOUT NATURAL LAWS

Do you take time to think and be introspective? Can you find more opportunities to look within yourself and think clearly? What is your plan?

How can you stop wearing your raincoat in the shower?

Respond to the quote:

"Tranquility leads to dynamic, creative thinking, and creative communication".

Is achieving tranquility your strength? If so, how do you do it? Can you teach it to others? How can you improve?

Consider The Law of the Farm. What seeds are you sowing?
What harvests are you reaping? What harvest is bountiful?
What would you like to change?

LET NATURE INCREASE YOUR SELF-AWARENESS

Dr. Covey stated that our ultimate freedom is deciding

"how anybody or anything outside ourselves will affect us."

If that is the standard, do you believe that you have achieved complete freedom? If not, what can you change?

Consider the quote:

> *"Until we see ourselves from the outside objectively, we will automatically project our motives onto other people."*

Have you seen this in your own life? If so, how do you believe it affects your relationships?

What are your thoughts on this quote by Dr. Covey:

"You can choose not to be offended, you can seek out your adversary and listen with empathy."

Have you ever been offended? In the future, how do you plan to handle a situation when you feel offended?

Respond to the quote:

> *"Anytime we think the problem is 'out there,' that thought is the problem."*

Why is it easier to be reactive than proactive in a situation? What is your personal tendency? How can you improve?

LET NATURE TEACH YOU HOW TO NURTURE RELATIONSHIPS

Do you put up unhealthy walls in your relationship? What are they? How can you tear them down?

Describe your family's unique and precious family culture.

Do you know someone who is a good listener? How do you feel when you're around this person? Do people feel the same around you? If not, how do you plan to change?

Is there a relationship you would like to nurture? If so, with whom? Why? What do you plan to do to nurture it?

LET NATURE GUIDE
YOUR CHOICES

How well do you adapt to change? Do you see change
as a good thing or a bad thing? Why?

List 3-4 principles you choose to live by. How do they help you achieve peace? Why did you choose these? What others would you like to work on?

Dr. Covey shared:

"Our choices reflect wisdom and lead to contribution."

What are your ideas about this statement?

Remember the idea of carrying your own weather? What ideas did you have when you read this story? How can you improve?

LET NATURE SHOW YOU HOW TO CELEBRATE DIVERSITY

What type of future do you dream of for yourself?
Your family? Your other important relationships?

Do you recognize relationships in your life where the whole is greater and better than the sum of the parts? Have you experienced the miracle of synergy? Can you find opportunities to expand that miracle into other relationships?

If you are in a relationship, how is your partner different from you? Do you treasure that difference? How and where can you find a way to celebrate more differences?

Do you feel peace in your life? Reflect on the quote by Dr. Covey:

"We can be examples and create peace in the world. And we grow our influence to help others discover peace."

What needs to happen in your life in order to be an example and create peace so others may discover it from you?

What is your plan?

CONCLUSION

What is your deepest learning from this book?
What insights did you gain?

What insight from this book would you like to share with others?
With whom will you share your learnings and insights?

What Chapter affected you the most? Why?

ACKNOWLEDGEMENTS

We gratefully acknowledge and express deep appreciation to the wonderful people who have made this project possible:

- To those whose lives and writings has come the wisdom of the ages. We have tried to learn from your legacy.

- To Chris McKenney of Mango Media, for his patience, insight, and guidance.

- To the members of the Franklin Covey team who helped throughout the entire process. For their significant contributions. In very challenging situations, they have demonstrated the character and competence we've tried to write about.

- Most of all, to our families and the families of the team, whose loving support has made all the difference.

CPSIA information can be obtained at www.ICGtesting.com
Printed in the USA
BVOW11s1648221115

427604BV00002B/2/P